Richard Doyle

The Foreign Tours of Messrs. Brown, Jones and Robinson

Being the History of what They Saw and Did in Belgium, Germany, Switzerland & Italy

Richard Doyle

The Foreign Tours of Messrs. Brown, Jones and Robinson
Being the History of what They Saw and Did in Belgium, Germany, Switzerland & Italy

ISBN/EAN: 9783337190927

Printed in Europe, USA, Canada, Australia, Japan

Cover: Foto ©Andreas Hilbeck / pixelio.de

More available books at **www.hansebooks.com**

The Foreign Tour of Messrs Brown, Jones, and Robinson

BEING THE HISTORY OF WHAT THEY SAW, AND DID IN BELGIUM, GERMANY, SWITZERLAND & ITALY.

by Richard Doyle.

NEW YORK.
D. APPLETON & CO.
1877.

LONDON.

THE MAIL TRAIN TO DOVER. BROWN, JONES, AND ROBINSON STARTING ON THEIR TRAVELS.

OSTEND.

AFTER A ROUGH PASSAGE, BROWN, JONES, AND ROBINSON ARE HERE SEEN LANDED AT OSTEND, SURROUNDED, AND A LITTLE BEWILDERED, BY THE NATIVES, WHO OVERWHELM THEM WITH ATTENTIONS—SEIZE THE LUGGAGE, THRUST CARDS INTO THEIR HANDS, DRAG THEM IN SEVERAL DIRECTIONS AT ONCE, ALL TALKING TOGETHER (WHICH PREVENTED THEIR DIRECTIONS BEING SO CLEAR AS THEY OTHERWISE WOULD HAVE BEEN)—AND, FINALLY, ALL EXPECTING MONEY!

THEY ARE AT THE DOUANE, WAITING FOR THE OFFICIALS TO SEARCH THE LUGGAGE.
ROBINSON AND JONES (ALARMED BY EXPRESSION OF BROWN'S COUNTENANCE).—" WHAT'S THE MATTER NOW?"
BROWN (IN A VOICE OF AGONY).—"I'VE LEFT THE KEY OF MY BAG AT HOME!"

OSTEND TO COLOGNE.

A SKETCH MADE AT MALINES.

HOW THEY SAW BELGIUM.

COLOGNE.

THE ARRIVAL AT COLOGNE.
TRAVELLERS PASSING THEIR EXAMINATION. IN THE FOREGROUND IS JONES'S PORTMANTEAU UNDERGOING THE "ORDEAL BY TOUCH."

MANNER AND CUSTOM OF THE PEOPLE, AS SEEN FROM THE RAILWAY BY BROWN, AND MADE A NOTE OF.

COLOGNE.

B. J. AND R., WHO TOOK THEIR PLACES ON THE ROOF THE BETTER TO COMMAND THE VIEW, ARE SEEN AT THE MOMENT WHEN THE IDEA OCCURRED TO THE TWO FORMER THAT THEY MIGHT POSSIBLY NOT "*FIT*" UNDER THE ARCHWAY. ROBINSON IS SO WRAPPED UP IN THOUGHT, AND A CIGAR, THAT HE IS UNCONSCIOUS OF ALL ELSE.

THIS REPRESENTS THE COLOGNE OMNIBUS ON ITS JOURNEY FROM THE STATION INTO THE CITY, WHEN STOPPED BY THE MILITARY, AND MADE TO "STAND AND DELIVER" THE PASSPORTS.

ARRIVAL AT THE HOTEL, AND FIRST COMING IN SIGHT OF THAT AMIABLE AND OBLIGING RACE, THE GERMAN WAITER. HE IS SMALL IN STATURE (SCARCELY THE SIZE OF LIFE, AS JONES REMARKED), AND REMAINS ALWAYS A BOY.

5

COLOGNE.

"SPEISE-SAAL" HOTEL, COLOGNE—ENTER BROWN, JONES, AND ROBINSON, FATIGUED, AND SOMEWHAT DISORDERED BY TRAVEL, AND "SO HUNGRY."

HOW AN AGENT OF JEAN MARIA FARINA ADDRESSED THEM, WHO WAS KIND ENOUGH TO PUT SOME OF THE CELEBRATED "EAU" UPON THEIR HANDKERCHIEFS, AND TO RECEIVE ORDERS FOR THE SAME.

COLOGNE.

THE REAL EAU DE COLOGNE, AND ITS EFFECT UPON THE NOSES OF THREE ILLUSTRIOUS INDIVIDUALS.

"KELLNER" PRESENTS THE BILL.

THEY "DO" COLOGNE CATHEDRAL.

COLOGNE TO BONN.

THE RAILWAY FROM COLOGNE TO BONN.—B. J. AND R. "JUST IN TIME."

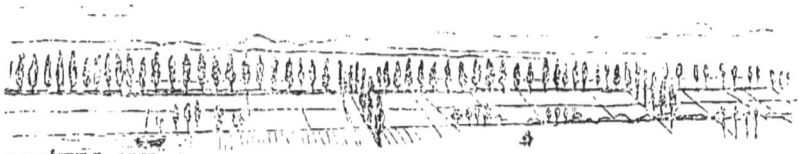

FIRST GLIMPSE OF RHINE SCENERY.

BONN.

JONES'S LITTLE ALL IS CONTAINED IN THIS SMALL PORTMANTEAU.

ROBINSON, ON THE CONTRARY, FINDS IT QUITE IMPOSSIBLE TO MOVE WITH LESS THAN THIS.

THIS SCENE REPRESENTS THE RHINE BOAT ABOUT TO START FROM BONN, AND PASSENGERS FROM THE RAILWAY EMBARKING. IN THE FOREGROUND AN ACCIDENT HAS OCCURRED, A PORTER HAVING UPSET THE LUGGAGE OF AN ENGLISH FAMILY, THE HEAD OF WHICH IS SALUTING HIM WITH THE NATIONAL "DAMN," WHILE THE COURIER OF THE PARTY EXPRESSES THE SAME IDEA IN GERMAN.

THE RHINE.

BROWN'S FIRST IMPRESSION OF THE RHINE.

From an ORIGINAL SKETCH *in the possession of his family*

HEADS OF THE NATIVES.

A Leaf from Brown's Sketch Book.

THE RHINE.

COMPANY ON BOARD THE RHINE BOAT.

AMONGST THEM WAS A TRAVELLING TUTOR, AND THREE YOUNG GENTLEMEN, HIS PUPILS. HE STOOD IN THE MIDST OF THEM SMILING BLANDLY, AN OPEN VOLUME IN HIS HAND, (PROBABLY A CLASSIC AUTHOR,) BETWEEN WHICH, AND HIS PUPILS, AND THE SCENERY, HE DIVIDED HIS ATTENTION IN ABOUT EQUAL PARTS. THERE WAS A SPECIMEN OF THE ENGLISH DRUMBLER, BIG, BURLY, AND AS IF IN DANGER OF CHOKING FROM THE TIGHTNESS OF HIS CRAVAT. EVERY ONE KNOWS HIM, HIS PLEASANT WAYS, AND HIS CONSTANT FLOW OF GOOD HUMOUR AND CHEERFULNESS; THAT IS HE, SITTING TO THE RIGHT. THERE WERE BESIDES, NUMEROUS YOUNG GENTLEMEN FROM THE UNIVERSITIES, FROM THE ARMY, FROM THE BAR, ALL WITH MORE OR LESS HAIR ON THEIR UPPER LIPS; AND THERE WAS A CAVALRY OFFICER OF THE RUSSIAN GUARD, AND A PROFESSOR, ON HIS WAY TO HEIDELBERG, AND LOOSE, DISHEVELLED, HAIRY, SMOKY YOUNG GERMANS, WITH LONG BEARDS, AND LONGER PIPES. AND THERE WAS A BRITISH NOBLEMAN, AND A BRITISH ALDERMAN, AND A BRITISH ALDERWOMAN; AND THERE WERE BRITISH LADIES WHOM I CAN'T DESCRIBE, BECAUSE THEY WORE THOSE "UGLY" THINGS WHICH PREVENT THEM BEING SEEN ; INTELLIGENT YOUNG AMERICANS ON THEIR WAY ALL OVER THE WORLD ; NUNS, WITH THEIR QUIET, HAPPY FACES ; RED REPUBLICANS FROM FRANKFORT, AND SNOBS FROM LONDON.

THE GREAT BRITON.

AS HE STOOD CONTEMPLATING THE RHINE-LAND, WONDERING IF IT WOULD BE POSSIBLE TO LIVE IN THAT COUNTRY ; AND CONSIDERING (SUPPOSING HE HAD ONE OF THOSE CASTLES, NOW) HOW MANY THOUSANDS A-YEAR ONE COULD DO IT WITH. THE SCENERY WOULD DO ; AND WITH ENGLISH INSTITUTIONS IT MIGHT BE MADE A GOOD THING OF.

N.B.—SEE LITTLE THINGS WHAT BROWN IS DOING.

THE RHINE.

EVEN THE NUN WAS NOT SAFE FROM BROWN. HE IS HERE SEEN TAKING HER OFF, IN A RAPID ACT OF SKETCHING.

B. J. AND R. HAD JUST BEGUN TO ENJOY THE SCENERY, WHEN, TO THEIR CONSTERNATION, WHO SHOULD APPEAR ON BOARD BUT THE "BORE," WHO INSTANTLY WAS DOWN UPON THEM. FOR THREE MORTAL HOURS HE ENTERTAINED THEM WITH FASHIONABLE INTELLIGENCE, ANECDOTES OF THE ARISTOCRACY, THE COURT CIRCULAR, BIRTHS, DEATHS, MARRIAGES, &C.

THE RHINE.

THIS WAS SUPPOSED TO BE AN M.P. TRAVELLING IN SEARCH OF "FACTS." HE IS GIVING BROWN HIS VIEWS; AND ALSO THE STATISTICS OF EVERYTHING.

A VIEW ON THE RHINE.

THE RHINE.

THE LONDON GENT UP THE RHINE.

HE IS TAKEN AT THE MOMENT WHEN EXPRESSING HIS OPINION THAT THE WHOLE CONCERN IS A "DO" AND A "SELL."

BRITISH FARMER AND SON IN FOREIGN PARTS.

THEY BOTH WORE A PERPETUAL GRIN AND STARE OF SURPRISE, JONES THOUGHT THAT THEY HAD TAKEN LEAVE OF ENGLAND AND THEIR SENSES AT ONCE, OWING TO THE WITHDRAWAL OF PROTECTION.

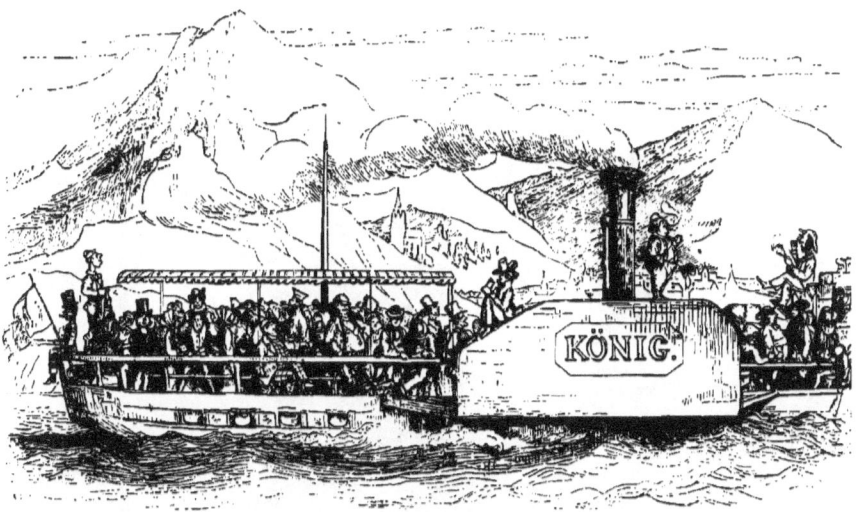

THE RHINE BOAT.

BROWN MAY BE SEEN SEATED THERE UPON THE PADDLE-BOX, RAPIDLY SKETCHING EVERY CHURCH, RUINED CASTLE, TOWN, OR OTHER OBJECT OF INTEREST ON EITHER BANK OF THE RIVER. THOSE ARE JONES AND ROBINSON, LEANING OVER THE SIDE OF THE BOAT BELOW HIM. OBSERVE, ALSO, THE STOUT PARTY WHO HAS CALLED FOR BRANDY-AND-WATER, AND WHOSE COUNTENANCE ALMOST LAPSES INTO A SMILE AS "KELLNER" APPROACHES WITH THE BEVERAGE. THE TUTOR, IT IS PLEASANT TO SEE, HAS AT LAST PUT HIS "CLASSIC" IN HIS POCKET, AND GIVES HIMSELF UP TO THE UNDIVIDED ENJOYMENT OF THE SCENE, WHILE HIS "YOUNG CHARGE" IS WRAPT IN CONTEMPLATION OF MECHANICAL SCIENCE AS EXEMPLIFIED IN THE STRUCTURE OF THE WHEEL. AND THAT MUST SURELY BE THE GENT WHO HAS SUCH A LOW OPINION OF THE BEAUTY OF THE RHINE-LAND, SEATED AT THE STERN OF THE BOAT WITH HIS LEGS DANGLING OVER THE RIVER. LET US HOPE THAT HE IS HAPPY NOW!

THE RHINE.

THE ENGLISH "MILORD" UPON THE RHINE.

HOW HAPPY HE LOOKS! HE DISLIKES THE HUM OF MEN, AND SITS ALL DAY SHUT UP IN HIS CARRIAGE READING THE LITERATURE OF HIS COUNTRY. HOW RUDE OF THOSE GERMANS TO BE LAUGHING AND JOKING SO NEAR HIS LORDSHIP!

PERFECT ENJOYMENT.

COBLENTZ.

INDIGNATION OF ROBINSON, AT SIGHT OF INADEQUATE WASHING APPARATUS. HE RANG THE BELL WITH SUCH VIOLENCE, THAT ALL THE WAITERS RUSHED IN, THINKING THAT THE HOTEL WAS ON FIRE, OR THAT A REVOLUTION HAD BROKEN OUT.

THERE HE STOOD, POINTING TO THE WATER, ABOUT HALF A PINT IN A BASIN THE SIZE OF A BREAKFAST CUP; AND IN A VOICE OF SUPPRESSED EMOTION, DEMANDING TO KNOW IF "DAS IST, ETC."

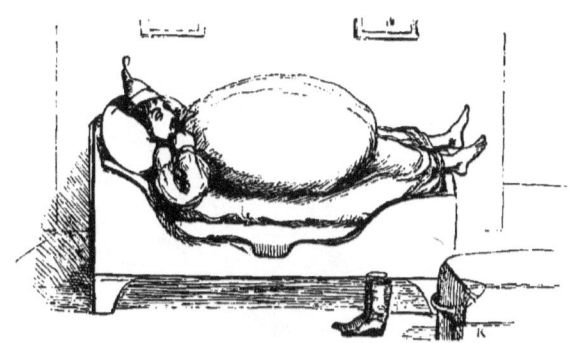

JONES'S NIGHT THOUGHTS.

"MAN WANTS BUT LITTLE HERE BELOW," BUT "WANTS THAT LITTLE LONG."

COBLENTZ.

IF YOU SHOULD FORGET THE NUMBER OF YOUR KEY AND ROOM (as BROWN *did on returning late from the theatre*), WHAT ARE YOU TO DO?

An Incident in the Life of Jones's Dog.

HOW THIS ANIMAL SEEMED TO HAVE IMBIBED COMMUNISTIC PRINCIPLES, AND HOW HE STOLE A SAUSAGE, AND HOW THE POPULATION ROSE LIKE ONE MAN, AND HUNTED HIM THROUGH THE TOWN.

COBLENTZ.

THE DOG HAVING OUTSTRIPPED THE POPULACE, PROCEEDS TO EAT THE SAUSAGE.

HAVING DONE SO, HE LOOKS STOUTER THAN HE DID, AND IS INCLINED TO REST. THE INHABITANTS, EAGER FOR VENGEANCE, SURROUND HIM, BUT ARE KEPT AT BAY BY THE EXPRESSION OF HIS COUNTENANCE.

ONE BURLY PEASANT HAVING THE HARDIHOOD TO APPROACH TOO NEAR, HE IS MADE AN EXAMPLE OF. *Exeunt omnes.*

THE RHINE.

BROWN, WITH NOBLE PERSEVERANCE, SITS UPON THE PADDLE-BOX, REGARDLESS OF THE STORM, AND SKETCHES THE CASTLES AND TOWNS, AS THE STEAM-BOAT PASSES THEM.

—TILL IN A MOMENT OF GRIEF HIS HAT AND SEVERAL SKETCHES WERE CARRIED OFF FOR EVER; AND THEN HE THOUGHT IT TIME TO GO BELOW.

THE RHINE.

HOW A CITIZEN OF THE UNITED STATES ADDRESSED BROWN; AND HOW HE PUT THE FOLLOWING QUESTIONS DURING THE FIRST FIVE MINUTES OF THEIR ACQUAINTANCE.
1. "WHERE ARE YOU GOING?"
2. "WHAT PLACE DO YOU HAIL FROM?"
3. "CONCLUDE YOU GO TOE FRANKFORT?"
4. "YOU'RE MR. BROWN, I RECKON?"
5. "WHAT NAMES DO YOUR FRIENDS GO BY?"

STATEMENTS MADE DURING THE SAME PERIOD.
1. "THIS HERE RHINE AIN'T MUCH BY THE SIDE OF OUR MISSISSIPPI."
2. "OLD EUROPE IS 'TARNALLY CHAWED UP."

BROWN'S HAT.

ROBINSON WAS VERY MERRY ABOUT THIS INCIDENT, AND BOTH HE AND JONES KEPT POKING FUN AT BROWN DURING THE REST OF THE DAY. THEY PARODIED THE WELL KNOWN SONG OF "MY HEART'S ON THE RHINE," SUBSTITUTING "MY HAT'S IN THE RHINE;"—(IT WAS VERY POOR STUFF, WE HAVE BEEN ASSURED BY BROWN) — AND THEY MADE POINTED ALLUSIONS TO THE NAME OF "WIDE-AWAKE."

THE ABOVE DRAWING IS FROM A RUDE SKETCH BY JONES.

THE SCENERY BECOMES MYSTERIOUS.

THEY NOW BECAME ENVELOPED IN WHAT SEEMED A COMBINATION OF FOG (LONDON NOVEMBER) AND MIST (SCOTCH). ONLY THINK OF THOSE TWO NATIONAL INSTITUTIONS GOING UP THE RHINE WITH THE REST OF THE FASHIONABLE WORLD. AT FIRST IT OBSCURED THE HILL TOPS, WITH THE RUINS THEREON; THEN THE VILLAGES AND VINEYARDS BELOW; AND FINALLY BOTH BANKS OF THE RIVER ENTIRELY DISAPPEARED. THE COMPANY ON BOARD THE STEAMBOAT DID NOT, AT THIS PERIOD, PRESENT THE MOST CHEERFUL ASPECT.

MAYENCE TO FRANKFORT.

"HOW ROBINSON'S FAVOURITE PORTMANTEAU, WHICH HE HAD FORGOTTEN TO LOCK, WAS DROPPED ACCIDENTALLY BY A PORTER WHILE CONVEYING IT TO THE OMNIBUS.

JONES HINTS TO ROBINSON THAT IT IS TIME TO GET UP.

FRANKFORT.

HOW THEY VISITED A "QUARTER" OF THE CITY OF FRANKFORT, AND WHAT THEY SAW THERE!

FRANKFORT.

ROBINSON HERE WROTE HIS CELEBRATED LETTER TO THE "TIMES," ON THE SUBJECT OF THE DEFICIENCY OF SOAP AND WATER, FROM WHICH, AS WE HAVE SEEN IN A FORMER PAGE, HE SUFFERED SO GRIEVOUSLY. IT WAS CONCEIVED IN TERMS OF INDIGNANT ELOQUENCE; AND DREW A TERRIBLE PICTURE OF THE STATE OF SOCIAL, POLITICAL, AND RELIGIOUS DEGRADATION INTO WHICH A COUNTRY MUST HAVE SUNK, WHERE SUCH THINGS COULD BE TOLERATED.

AS THEY WALKED THROUGH THE TOWN, BENT UPON SEEING THE ARIADNE, AND UNCONSCIOUS OF DANGER, SUDDENLY AN OBJECT APPEARED IN SIGHT THAT FILLED THEM WITH TERROR. IT WAS THE "BORE!" STEPPING JAUNTILY ALONG ON THE OTHER SIDE OF THE STREET. TO HESITATE WAS TO BE LOST! SO THEY PLUNGED INTO THE NEAREST SHOP FOR PROTECTION, AND STOOD THERE BREATHLESS WITH EXPECTATION AND FEAR. PRESENTLY JONES—PUTTING HIS HEAD VERY GRADUALLY OUT—RECONNOITRED, AND FINDING ALL SAFE THEY RESUMED THEIR WAY.

ROBINSON THINKS IT "THE THING" TO ENCOURAGE NATIVE INDUSTRY WHEREVER HE GOES, AND SO BUYS A GERMAN PIPE.

HEIDELBERG.

"KELLNER!"

WHILE BROWN, JONES, AND ROBINSON SUPPED, A PARTY OF PHILOSOPHERS CARRY ON AN ÆSTHETICAL DISCUSSION, WITH AN ACCOMPANIMENT OF PIPES AND BEER.

HEIDELBERG.

"* * * THE NIGHT WAS BEAUTIFUL, SO WE DETERMINED AFTER SUPPER TO HAVE A LOOK AT THE CELEBRATED CASTLE—JONES AND I DID, THAT IS TO SAY, FOR ROBINSON WAS SO FATIGUED WITH TRAVEL THAT HE DECLINED MOVING, MUTTERING SOMETHING ABOUT 'CASTLE CAN WAIT.' WE ASCENDED; THE MOON SHONE BRIGHTLY THROUGH THE RUINS, AND BATHED THE LANDSCAPE IN ITS SILVERY LIGHT, THE BEAUTIFUL NECKAR FLOWING AT OUR FEET. UNDER US LAY THE TOWN, A THOUSAND LIGHTS TWINKLING IN THE STILLNESS." * * "SUDDENLY, TO OUR HORROR, THERE APPEARED UPON THE TERRACE 'THE BORE!'"—*Extract from Brown's Journal.*

"AT LAST HE LEFT US. BUT NOT BEFORE HE HAD TAKEN FROM HIS POCKET A LETTER RECEIVED THAT MORNING FROM GREEN ('YOU KNOW GREEN, OF COURSE,' HE SAID, 'EVERYBODY DOES'), AND READ IT ALOUD FROM BEGINNING TO END. IT TOLD OF A 'GOOD THING' SAID AT THE CLUB BY SMITH; AND OF TWO MARRIAGES, AND A DUEL LIKELY TO COME OFF, BESIDES SEVERAL INTERESTING PARTICULARS REGARDING THE WINNER OF THE ST. LEGER."—*Ibid.*

WHEN JONES AND BROWN WERE LEFT ONCE MORE ALONE, THEY WANDERED AND PONDERED AMONGST THE RUINS, AND MORALISED OVER THE INSTABILITY OF THINGS—THEY WERE EVEN BECOMING SENTIMENTAL—WHEN, SUDDENLY, A TERRIFIC SOUND WAS HEARD—LIKE THE BARKING OF A DOG—AND THE NEXT MOMENT THE ANIMAL HIMSELF WAS SEEN EMERGING FROM THE DARKNESS, AND MAKING TOWARDS THEM AT THE TOP OF HIS SPEED. THEY TURNED AND FLED!

HEIDELBERG.

MEETING BY MOONLIGHT.

ROBINSON, AFTER THE DEPARTURE OF JONES AND BROWN, SEATED HIMSELF BEFORE THE FIRE AND FELL FAST ASLEEP.

HEIDELBERG.

HE CONTINUED IN THAT STATE, NOTWITHSTANDING THAT THE PHILOSOPHERS BECAME VERY NOISY, AND EVEN WARLIKE.

—AND ALTHOUGH—AFTER THE LATTER HAD RETIRED (FORTUNATELY WITHOUT COMING TO BLOWS)—HIS CHAIR TOPPLED OVER, HE QUIETLY ASSUMED A HORIZONTAL POSITION.

FANCY THE FEELINGS OF JONES AND BROWN ON RETURNING, AND FINDING THEIR FRIEND LYING ON HIS BACK UPON THE FLOOR, SNORING!

HEIDELBERG.

THEY LIFTED HIM UP, AND CARRIED HIM OFF TO BED.

NEXT MORNING THEY ENTERTAINED ROBINSON WITH A THRILLING ACCOUNT OF THE DANGERS OF THEIR EXPEDITION, IN WHICH THAT DREADFUL DOG FILLED A VERY LARGE SPACE.

THE ABOVE WILL GIVE SOME FAINT IDEA OF WHAT THEY PICTURED TO THEMSELVES (AND TO ROBINSON).

THE REVIEW.

Brown, Jones, and Robinson have arrived at ——, the capital of ——, a small German state (we won't say which, as it would be giving it an undue distinction, and might offend the others).

They have been received with distinguished consideration, the "local" paper having announced their arrival as Count Robinson, Sir Brown, and the Rev. Jones. They have been invited to be present at a grand review, and Robinson—who amongst other necessaries in those portmanteaus of his, carried a uniform as Captain of Yeomanry—thought that this was just the proper occasion to appear in it. Accordingly, he rode on to the ground upon a charger (hired), in the character of a warrior, with a solemnity of countenance befitting the scene and his country, and accompanied by Jones (also mounted), but in the costume of an ordinary individual of the period. Brown preferred going on foot. That is Robinson in the centre. Just at the time when he ought to be riding up the line, inspecting the troops with the Grand Duke and his staff—his horse (a "disgusting brute," as Robinson afterwards described him, "who could not have been in the habit of carrying gentlemen") suddenly stood on his hind legs, in the very middle of the field, so that his rider was forced to cling on to him in an absurd manner, in full view of the army, the people, and the court.

He, at that moment earnestly desired that the earth might open and swallow him.

KEY TO THE CARTOON.

1. Robinson. 2. The Grand Duke. 3. The Crown Prince. 4. The Rest of the Serene Family. 5. Mr. Jones. 6. The Population. 7. Mr. Jones's Dog. 8. Mr. Brown. 9. The Army. 10. Distant View of the Capital. 11. Foreign Visitors. 12. Monument to late Duke.

BADEN.

A SCENE AT BADEN

THE RIGHT OF SEARCH.

BADEN.

Of the Adventure that befel Jones.

I.

JONES'S DOG HAVING COME UPON A SENTINEL, AND STRUCK, PERHAPS, BY HIS SMALL SIZE COMPARED WITH THE SENTINELS HE IS USED TO, COMMENCES TO SAY, "BOW!—WOW!—WOW!—WEW—U—U!"
THE SOLDIER, OFFENDED BY THESE REMARKS, PRESENTS FOR THE ANIMAL'S CONSIDERATION, THE POINT OF HIS BAYONET.

II.

JONES EXPOSTULATES, WITH THAT FREEDOM OF SPEECH WHICH IS THE BIRTHRIGHT OF EVERY ENGLISHMAN.

III.

BUT OBTAINING NO SATISFACTION, CALLS ON THE MISERABLE FOREIGNER TO "COME ON."

BADEN.

IV.

FIRST (AND LAST) ROUND.—THE SOLDIER DID "COME ON," FROWNING. JONES RECEIVED HIM, SMILING.—THE SOLDIER MADE PLAY WITH HIS MUSKET: JONES PUT IN HIS LEFT. THEY CLOSED, AND A TERRIFIC STRUGGLE ENSUED, IN THE COURSE OF WHICH JONES GOT HIS ADVERSARY'S "NOB" INTO "CHANCERY."

V.

THE SOLDIER, AT THIS POINT, UNABLE TO USE HIS ARMS, TOOK TO HIS LEGS, AND ADMINISTERED A SERIES OF KICKS UPON THE SHINS OF JONES, WHO IN RETURN SEIZED HIM, LIFTED HIM IN THE AIR, AND THREW HIM.

VI.

THEN, CONSIDERING THAT JUSTICE AND THE HONOUR OF HIS COUNTRY WERE ALIKE SATISFIED, HE RETIRED, LEAVING THE BODY OF HIS ANTAGONIST ON THE FIELD.

VII.

SHOWS THE "BODY," ON DISCOVERING THAT LIFE WAS NOT EXTINCT, ATTEMPTING TO RISE.

P.S.—HE WAS LAST SEEN MAKING FRANTIC EFFORTS TO REGAIN HIS FEET, AND SEEMINGLY PREVENTED FROM DOING SO BY THE WEIGHT OF HIS KNAPSACK, AND OTHER ACCOUTREMENTS.

BADEN.

VIII.

JONES WAS LATE AT BREAKFAST; HE FOUND ROBINSON READING "GALIGNANI," AND BROWN LOOKING OUT OF WINDOW, AND AFTER GIVING THEM AN AMUSING ACCOUNT OF THE FUN HE HAD HAD, WAS JUST SITTING DOWN TO THE TABLE, WHEN BROWN SHOUTED OUT, "BY JOVE, THERE IS A REGIMENT OF SOLDIERS COMING DOWN THE STREET!"

IX.

AT FIRST JONES WAS INCREDULOUS; BUT PRESENTLY BROWN, HIS HAIR STANDING ON END, RUSHED TOWARDS HIM, AND IN A VOICE OF AGONY, CRIED, "AS SURE AS WE ARE ALIVE THEY HAVE STOPPED IN FRONT OF THE HOUSE, AND THE *OFFICER IS COMING IN!*"

BADEN.

X.

IT WAS TOO TRUE. THE SOLDIERS HAD COME TO LOOK AFTER THE ENGLISHMAN WHO HAD ATTACKED AND BEATEN THEIR COMRADE.

XI.

AFTER A FEW MOMENTS OF BREATHLESS SUSPENSE, THE OFFICER ENTERS—JONES STANDS LIKE A MAN ABOUT TO STRUGGLE WITH ADVERSITY.

BADEN.

XII.
NEVERTHELESS HE IS ARRESTED AND MARCHED OFF.

XIII.
ROBINSON, IN AGONY, CALLS FOR HIS COAT AND HAT, "FOR," AS HE CRIED OUT TO BROWN, "NOT A MOMENT IS TO BE LOST IN ENDEAVOURING TO SEE THE BRITISH MINISTER."

BADEN TO BASLE.

XIV.

THEY GAIN AN AUDIENCE OF HIS EXCELLENCY THE BRITISH MINISTER, AND ASK HIS INTERFERENCE IN BEHALF OF A PERSECUTED COUNTRYMAN.

WE ARE HAPPY TO ADD THAT THE INTERFERENCE WAS QUITE SUCCESSFUL. JONES WAS LIBERATED IMMEDIATELY, AND SHORTLY AFTERWARDS THE BRITISH MINISTER FOR FOREIGN AFFAIRS, IN A DESPATCH TO THE GERMAN MINISTER FOR THE SAME, EXPRESSED HIS CONVICTION THAT "THE WHOLE CIVILISED WORLD REPROBATED, WITH ONE VOICE, A SYSTEM AT ONCE TYRANNICAL AND CRUEL, A REMNANT OF THE DARKEST AGES OF MAN'S HISTORY, AND UTTERLY UNWORTHY OF THE PRESENT ERA OF PROGRESS AND ENLIGHTENMENT."

OUR FRIENDS WERE ADVISED, HOWEVER, TO LEAVE THE COUNTRY AS SOON AND AS QUIETLY AS POSSIBLE. THEY DEPARTED ACCORDINGLY.

HEAD-DRESSES OF PEASANTRY. A SKETCH ON THE ROAD TO BASLE.

BADEN TO BASLE.

HOW BROWN AND JONES WENT IN A THIRD CLASS CARRIAGE (ROBINSON WOULD NOT; IT DID NOT SEEM "RESPECTABLE"), THAT THEY MIGHT SEE THE NATIVES, AND HOW B. DREW THE PORTRAIT OF ONE, TO HER EVIDENT DISSATISFACTION.

THE OMNIBUS BESIEGED AND TAKEN BY STORM.

BASLE.

SCENE FROM THE ROAD, NEAR BASLE.

"THE HEIGHT OF THE OMNIBUSES IS QUITE DISGUSTING."—*Extract from unpublished documents in possession of* ROBINSON, *who himself fell in the mud, while climbing from the roof of one of those vehicles.*

STORKS' NEST, BASLE.

SWITZERLAND.

BOAT STATION ON THE LAKE OF LUCERNE; AS SKETCHED BY BROWN FROM THE STEAMER.

ACCORDING TO THE GUIDE-BOOK, THE PAINTINGS ON THE WALL REPRESENT FURST, STAUFFACH, AND MELCHTHAL, SWEARING TO LIBERATE THEIR COUNTRY; BUT JONES SAID HE BELIEVED THEM TO BE PORTRAITS OF A MEDIÆVAL SWISS BROWN, JONES, AND ROBINSON, IN THE ACT OF VOWING ETERNAL FRIENDSHIP.

THE SAFEST WAY OF COMING DOWN A MOUNTAIN.

SWITZERLAND.

"WE GOT OUT OF THE DILIGENCE (AT A TIME WHEN IT WAS OBLIGED TO GO VERY SLOWLY), IN ORDER TO MAKE AN EXCURSION ON FOOT IN SEARCH OF THE PICTURESQUE, BEING TOLD THAT WE MIGHT MEET THE CARRIAGE AT A CERTAIN POINT, ABOUT A MILE FURTHER ON. WE SAW MANY MAGNIFICENT VIEWS, AND DID A GREAT DEAL OF WHAT MIGHT BE CALLED ROUGH WALKING; BUT PERHAPS THE THING THAT STRUCK US MOST WAS, THAT ON EMERGING AT THE APPOINTED SPOT FOR REJOINING THE DILIGENCE, WE BEHELD IT A SPECK IN THE DISTANCE, JUST DEPARTING OUT OF SIGHT."—*Extract from Jones's Journal.*

THE SEVEN AGES OF ROBINSON'S BEARD.

SWITZERLAND.

WHAT ARE THEY TO DO NOW?

SWITZERLAND.

DESCENT OF THE ST. GOTHARD.
HAVING TAKEN THEIR PLACES ON THE OUTSIDE OF THE DILIGENCE, BROWN, JONES, AND ROBINSON CAN THE BETTER ENJOY THE GRANDEUR OF THE SCENERY.

SWITZERLAND.

THEY SEE ITALY IN THE DISTANCE.

PILGRIMS COMING *DOWN* THE
"HILL OF DIFFICULTY."

A MEETING ON THE MOUNTAIN.

ITALY.

BREAKFAST AT BELLINZONA.

IT WAS THEIR FIRST DAY IN ITALY, AND HOW THEY DID ENJOY IT! THE REPAST WAS SERVED IN A STONE SUMMER-HOUSE ATTACHED TO THE HOTEL. THE SUN WAS SO BRIGHT, AND SO HOT; THE SKY WAS SO BLUE, THE VEGETATION SO GREEN, THE MOUNTAINS SO PURPLE, THE GRAPES SO LARGE, AND EVERYTHING SO BEAUTIFUL, THAT BROWN AND JONES BOTH DECIDED THAT THE SCENE FULLY REALISED ALL THEIR IMAGININGS OF ITALY. ROBINSON WAS ENTHUSIASTIC, TOO, AT FIRST, AND WAS BEGINNING TO SAY SOMETHING ABOUT "ITALIA, O ITALIA," WHEN HIS EYE LIT UPON A GREEN LIZARD RUNNING UP THE WALL. FROM THAT MOMENT HE WAS MORE SUBDUED.

HOW THEY GOT ROBINSON UP THE HILLS.

ITALIAN LAKES.

THEY LAND UPON AUSTRIAN TERRITORY EN ROUTE FOR MILAN. WHILE THE "PROPER OFFICER" TAKES POSSESSION OF THEIR PASSPORTS. THE WHOLE AVAILABLE POPULATION POUNCES UPON THE LUGGAGE, AND, AFTER APPORTIONING IT INTO "SMALL ALLOTMENTS," CARRIES IT OFF TO THE CUSTOM HOUSE.

THE OFFICIAL HERE IS SEEN "POINTING" ON THE SCENT (AS HE THINKS) OF CONTRABAND GOODS IN ONE OF ROBINSON'S PORTMANTEAUS. HE DID NOT "FIND," BUT IN THE HUNT, TOSSED R.'S "THINGS" DREADFULLY. BROWN REVENGED THE WRONGS OF SELF AND FRIENDS, BY TAKING A FULL LENGTH, ON THE SPOT, OF THAT IMPOSING ADMINISTRATOR, WHO STANDS OVER THERE, WITH THE PASSPORTS IN HIS HAND.

ITALIAN LAKES.

"EXCELSIOR!"

"BUON GIORNO."

AN ITALIAN VIEW.

ITALIAN LAKES.

EVENING IN THE LAGO MAGGIORE.

"'KNOWEST THOU THE LAND' WHERE THE GRAPES ARE AS PLENTIFUL AS BLACKBERRIES IN ENGLAND; AND WHERE ONE HAS ONLY TO STOP A MINUTE AT THE ROADSIDE, AND PULL NO END OF 'EM. O 'TIS THERE! 'TIS THERE! ETC."—*Robinson's Letters to his Kinsfolk.*

ITALIAN LAKES.

MARIE.

OH ! MARIE OF THE LAGO D'ORTA, MAID OF THE INN, AND MOST BEAUTIFUL OF WAITRESSES, HOW WELL DO I REMEMBER THEE! HOW GRACEFUL WERE ALL THY MOVEMENTS ; WHAT NATURAL EASE, TOGETHER WITH WHAT A DIGNIFIED RESERVE ; —HOW TRULY A LADY WERT THOU ! YOU DID NOT KNOW IT, BUT WHEN YOU WAITED UPON US, I ALWAYS FELT INCLINED TO JUMP UP FROM MY CHAIR, AND OPEN THE DOOR FOR YOU— TO TAKE THE DISHES FROM YOUR HANDS, — TO ASK YOU RESPECTFULLY TO BE SEATED,—TO WAIT UPON YOU IN FACT. AND O ! HOW I DID DETEST THAT WICKED OLD LANDLADY, YOUR MISTRESS, WHO USED TO BULLY AND SCOLD YOU. AND I WONDER WHETHER YOU REMEMBER ME.—*From a MS., very rare, in possession of Brown.*

THIS PICTURE REPRESENTS BROWN AS HE APPEARED, HIS FEELINGS BEING "TOO MANY FOR HIM," ON HEARING THAT ELDERLY SHE-DRAGON, THE LANDLADY, VENTING HER ILL-HUMOUR UPON THE GENTLE MARIE. HE STOLE OUT OF THE DINING-ROOM, LOOKED OVER INTO THE YARD, AND THERE BEHELD THE FURIOUS OLD FEMALE SHAKING HER FIST, AND POURING FORTH A TORRENT OF ABUSE. BROWN WAS NOT NATURALLY OF A SAVAGE TEMPERAMENT, BUT AT THAT MOMENT HE FELT THAT HE COULD HAVE—BUT IT IS BEST NOT TO SAY WHAT HE COULD HAVE DONE —IT WAS TOO TERRIBLE FOR PUBLICATION IN THESE PAGES.

A BOAT AT ORTA.

ITALIAN LAKES.

A MOUNTAIN WALK.
ROBINSON, WITH WARMTH, AND SOME DISTANCE BEHIND,—"WHAT IS THE USE OF GOING ON AT THAT RATE?"

POOR JONES! WHO WOULD HAVE THOUGHT HE COULD EVER BE TIRED!

ITALIAN LAKES.

PLEASANT.

ITALIAN LAKES.

THE ACCIDENT THAT BEFELL ROBINSON.—No. 1.

THE ACCIDENT THAT BEFELL ROBINSON.—No. 2.

ROBINSON RETIRES FOR THE NIGHT.
TO PREVENT ANXIETY, WE HAD BETTER STATE THAT HE IS TIRED—NOTHING ELSE.

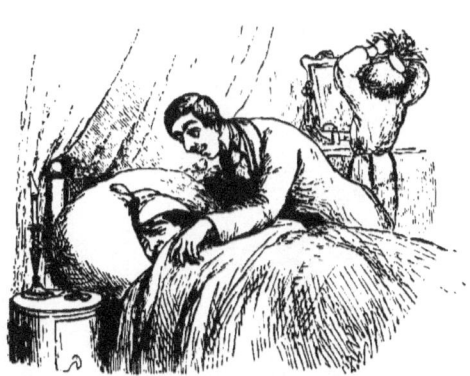

"NOW DO, ROBINSON, JUMP UP LIKE A GOOD FELLOW; WE OUGHT TO BE STARTING NOW—AND THINK HOW PLEASANT IT WILL BE, ONCE YOU ARE UP!"

VARALLO.

THE INN.

HOW BROWN, RETURNING FROM SKETCHING, WAS BESET BY BEGGARS IN A LONELY PLACE.

MILAN.

THEY PAY A VISIT TO THE MARIONETTE THEATRE.

A SNOB THEY SAW WRITING HIS NAME UPON ROOF OF MILAN CATHEDRAL.

ENLIGHTENED BEHAVIOUR IN A FOREIGN CHURCH.
WE ARE HAPPY TO SAY, THAT B. J. AND R. HAD NO CONNECTION WITH THE ABOVE PARTY.

MILAN.

ROBINSON'S DETERMINATION TO LET HIS BEARD GROW "NATURALLY," HAD AN ABSURD RESULT, THE HAIR GROWING IN VIOLENT AND ABRUPT CROPS IN SOME PLACES, AND NOT AT ALL IN OTHERS; SO THAT JONES, WHO WAS SENSITIVE ABOUT APPEARANCES, (AND WHOSE OWN MOUSTACHE WAS DOING BEAUTIFULLY,) INSISTED AT LAST UPON R.'S BEING SHAVED, WHICH EVENT ACCORDINGLY TOOK PLACE IN THE CITY OF MILAN. IT WAS WELL THAT ROBINSON CONSENTED, FOR THE BARBER EYED HIM EAGERLY, AND AS IF HE WOULD SPRING UPON HIM AND SHAVE HIM BY FORCE.

CAFÉ MILAN.—SUDDEN AND UNEXPECTED ARRIVAL OF DISTINGUISHED FOREIGNERS

THE MOMENT WE SEATED OURSELVES IN A CAFÉ, AN AWFUL GROUP OF BEGGARS STOOD BEFORE US—SO SUDDENLY THAT THEY APPEARED TO HAVE COME UP THROUGH A TRAP-DOOR—AND DEMANDED ALMS. THEY WOULD NOT GO WITHOUT MONEY, AND WHEN THEY GOT IT THEY TOOK IT AS A RIGHT. IT WOULD NOT DO FOR ONE OF US TO "SETTLE" WITH THEM FOR THE WHOLE PARTY, FOR NO SOONER HAD I GIVEN THEM A COIN THAN THEY TURNED TO JONES, AND WHEN DONE WITH HIM, COOLLY SET UPON ROBINSON. THE INSTANT ONE TRIBE DEPARTED, A FRESH RELAIS ARRIVED, SO THAT THERE WAS A CONSTANT SUPPLY (OF BEGGARS) AND DEMAND (ON OUR PURSES).

NO PLACE SEEMED SAFE: IN THE MOST MAGNIFICENT AND LUXURIOUSLY-DECORATED CAFÉS THEY HAD PERFECT RIGHT OF WAY, THE CONTRAST BETWEEN THE RICH GILDING, GLASS, FOUNTAINS, ETC., OF THE ONE, AND THE RAGS, DIRT, AND DRAMATICALLY GOT-UP HORRORS OF THE OTHER BEING PICTURESQUE, BUT CERTAINLY NOT PLEASANT; AND YET, AS JONES REMARKED, THEY SAY THIS COUNTRY HAS NOT FREE INSTITUTIONS.

VERONA.

THE AMPHITHEATRE, VERONA.

JONES ASKS ROBINSON, WHETHER HE "SEES BEFORE HIM THE GLADIATOR DIE?" BUT ROBINSON MAINTAINS A DIGNIFIED SILENCE.

AUSTRIAN DETECTIVE STOPS BROWN TO EXAMINE HIS SKETCHING STOOL. IT PUZZLES HIM. THERE IS AN AIR OF MYSTERY ABOUT IT. IT MIGHT POSSIBLY BE A WEAPON TO BE USED FOR POLITICAL PURPOSES, OR AN INFERNAL MACHINE! WHO KNOWS? ON THE WHOLE, HE THINKS HE HAD BETTER DETAIN IT.

VERONA.

SCENE.—DISCOVERS BROWN SKETCHING.
ENTER THE AUSTRIAN ARMY. THEY ADVANCE UPON HIM, THEY THINK HE IS TAKING THE FORTIFICATIONS.

ROBINSON, WHO IS MUCH GIVEN TO QUOTATION, IS, AT THE VERY MOMENT, LANGUIDLY RECITING THE LINES:—

"AM I IN ITALY? IS THIS THE MINCIUS?
AND THOSE THE DISTANT TURRETS OF VERONA?
AND SHALL I SUP WHERE JULIET AT THE MASQUE
SAW HER LOVED MONTAGUE!"—ETC., ETC.

VERONA.

NOT BEING FAMILIAR WITH THE GERMAN, OR THE CROATIAN LANGUAGE, BROWN IS HELPLESS. HE PROTESTS HIS INNOCENCE, BUT THE MILITARY DON'T UNDERSTAND HIM. THEY SEE TREASON IN HIS HAT, WHICH IS OF AN ILLEGAL SHAPE, AND THEY ARREST HIM.

JONES AND ROBINSON APPEAR, TO THE SURPRISE OF THE MILITARY, AND RELIEF OF BROWN.

VERONA.

BROWN, QUITE RESIGNED, WALKS QUIETLY TO MEET HIS FATE. JONES PLUNGES VIOLENTLY, BUT IS FINALLY OVERCOME. ROBINSON RESISTS PASSIVELY, AND IS ACCORDINGLY DRAGGED ALONG.

SKETCHES FOUND UPON BROWN.

VERONA.

THEY ARE BROUGHT BEFORE THE GOVERNOR. THAT IS HE SEATED AT THE TABLE, THE SOLDIERS SHOWING HIM THE LIBELLOUS REPRESENTATIONS OF THE CROATS FOUND IN BROWN'S PORTFOLIO. THE LATTER EXPECTS TO BE ORDERED FOR INSTANT EXECUTION; BUT JONES ASSUMES AN AIR OF GREAT DIGNITY, AND SAYS, "*Civis Romanus sum.*"

THE GOVERNOR, FIELD-MARSHAL LIEUTENANT COUNT BROWN, OF THE IMPERIAL SERVICE, DISCOVERS IN HIS PRISONER A NEAR RELATION OF HIS OWN; AND OUR FRIEND IS INSTANTLY LOCKED IN THE EMBRACE OF THAT DISTINGUISHED WARRIOR. JONES REMARKED "ALL'S WELL THAT ENDS WELL;" AND ROBINSON, GREATLY RELIEVED, BROKE OUT WITH:—

"THUS MAY EACH" NEPHEW "WHOM CHANCE DIRECTS,
FIND AN" UNCLE "WHEN HE LEAST EXPECTS."

VENICE.

EXAMINATION OF PASSPORTS.

HOTEL

VENICE.

MODERN VENETIAN TROUBADOURS.
AN EVENING SCENE BEFORE THE CAFÉ FLORAIN. PIAZZA SAN MARCO.

BROWN AT THIS PERIOD UNDERTOOK, AT THE URGENT REQUEST OF JONES AND ROBINSON, TO SETTLE THE ACCOUNTS OF THE PARTY, WHICH HAD BECOME COMPLICATED OWING TO THAT PERPLEXING "MEDIUM," TO THOSE UNUSED TO IT, THE AUSTRIAN PAPER MONEY.
THIS IS A FAITHFUL PICTURE OF THE UNFORTUNATE MAN AS HE SAT, IN THE SOLITUDE OF HIS CHAMBER, UNTIL A LATE HOUR OF THE NIGHT, DRAWING UP THE "FINANCIAL" STATEMENT.

VENICE.

ROBINSON (solo).—"I STOOD IN VENICE," ETC.; JONES AND BROWN, HAVING HEARD SOMETHING LIKE IT BEFORE HAVE WALKED ON A LITTLE WAY.
Reflection made by BROWN.—WHY DO PEOPLE WHEN REPEATING POETRY ALWAYS LOOK UNHAPPY?

ENJOYMENT!
A SCENE UPON THE GRAND CANAL.

VENICE.

THE THEATRE MALIBRAN.

THE ENTERTAINMENT COMMENCED AT 5 P.M., AND LASTED TILL 7. IT CONSISTED OF A MELODRAMA, FULL OF AWFUL CRIMES, AND THE MOST PATHETIC SENTIMENT. THE AUDIENCE, CHIEFLY COMPOSED OF "THE PEOPLE," WAS, FROM BEGINNING TO END, IN AN EXTRAORDINARY STATE OF EXCITEMENT, FIZZING, LIKE THE PERPETUAL GOING OFF OF SODA-WATER. THE THEATRE WAS LIGHTED (?) BY ABOUT FOUR OIL LAMPS; AND SUCH WAS THE DARKNESS, THAT OUR TRAVELLERS—WHO MAY BE SEEN, PERHAPS, THROUGH THE "DIM OBSCURE," UP IN A PRIVATE BOX—COULD SCARCELY DISCERN ANYTHING BUT THE WHITE UNIFORM AND GLITTERING BAYONET OF AN AUSTRIAN SENTINEL IN THE PIT.

BROWN RETIRED TO REST.

A NIGHT IN VENICE.

MISERY.

NOTE.—If the Musquitos appear rather large in this and the following scenes, let it be remembered that in the "heroic" it was a principle of many of the great painters to exaggerate the "parts."

DESPERATION.

MOMENTARY RELIEF.

A NIGHT IN VENICE.

MADNESS!

BELL!!

BOOTS!!!

DESPAIR!!!!

VENICE.

THE ACCADEMIA.

GONDOLA ON THE LAGOON.

SENTIMENT SPOKEN BY ROBINSON, WITH MARKS OF ADHESION FROM BROWN AND JONES.
"OH, IF THERE BE AN ELYSIUM ON EARTH, IT IS THIS, IT IS THIS!!"

VENICE.

The Accademia.

SCENE I.

SCENE II.

BROWN (SOLILOQUY). —"THIS IS PLEASANT! TO BE QUITE ALONE HERE (DAB), SURROUNDED BY THESE MAGNIFICENT WORKS (DAB, DAB, DAB), AND EVERYTHING SO QUIET TOO—NOTHING TO DISTURB ONE." (DAB)—AFTER A PAUSE. "I WONDER WHAT JONES AND ROBINSON ARE DOING (DAB, SPLASH)—LYING AT FULL LENGTH IN A GONDOLA, I DARE SAY—SMOKING (DAB). I THINK I COULD SPEND MY LIFE IN THIS PLACE" (DAB, DAB).

"IT IS DIFFICULT TO SAY WHICH IS THE GREATEST PLEASURE, (ANOTHER DAB,) COPYING THESE SPLENDID PICTURES, OR PAINTING FROM NATURE, THOSE BEAUTIFUL BLUE SKIES AND CRUMBLING OLD PICTURESQUE PALACES, OUTSIDE."

(SINGS)— "'HOW HAPPY COULD I BE WITH EITHER.'" (PROLONGED PAUSE, AND GREAT PLAY WITH BRUSH)—"OH! THAT SUNSET LAST EVENING! AS WE LAY OUT IN OUR GONDOLA UPON THE PERFECTLY CALM WATERS, BY THE ARMENIAN CONVENT, AND WATCHED THE SUN SLOWLY GOING DOWN BEHIND THE DISTANT TOWERS AND SPIRES OF THE 'CITY OF THE SEA'—ONE MASS OF GOLD SPREADING ALL OVER THE WEST!" * * "OH! THOSE CLOUDS! (ANOTHER PAUSE) AH! THAT WAS HAPPINESS. ONE SUCH HOUR IS WORTH — LET ME SEE — HOW MANY YEARS OF ONE'S LIFE!" * * AND YET THIS IS—"

HE IS SET UPON AND SURROUNDED BY AN ENGLISH FAMILY, AND THE FOLLOWING DIALOGUE ENSUES:—

THE MAMMA.—"WHAT A DELIGHTFUL OCCUPATION, TO BE SURE."

YOUNG LADY (IN A WHISPER).—"HE IS COPYING THE TINTORET."

YOUTHFUL SON AND HEIR (WITH CONFIDENCE).—"NO, HE AIN'T; HE'S DOING THAT STUNNING BIG ONE WITH THE RAINBOW, AND THREE RIVER GODS."

SECOND YOUNG LADY.—"IT'S SWEETLY PRETTY, ISN'T IT!"

PAPA (A BRITISH MERCHANT, AND OF A PRACTICAL TURN).—"VERY GOOD — V-E-R-Y GOOD. AHEM! NOW I WONDER WHAT ONE COULD MAKE A YEAR BY THAT KIND OF THING."

YOUNG MAN (WITH GLASS IN HIS EYE).—"SLOW, I SHOULD THINK."

AT THIS POINT BROWN'S ATTENTION WAS ATTRACTED TO A SCUFFLE GOING ON BEHIND HIM AMONGST THE JUNIOR MEMBERS OF THE PARTY. TWO OF THE LITTLE INNOCENTS HAD TAKEN A FANCY TO THE SAME DRAWING (A COPY OF HIS FAVOURITE JOHN BELLINO), AND AFTER A BRIEF, BUT FIERCE STRUGGLE FOR POSSESSION, HAD SETTLED THE DIFFICULTY BY TEARING IT IN TWO. —(PARTY RETIRES RATHER PRECIPITATELY.)

TRIESTE TO VIENNA.

SKETCH MADE BY BROWN AT TRIESTE.
NOTE.—If any one doubts the fact, Jones and Robinson are ready to make affidavit of it.

ROBINSON SEARCHED AND INDIGNANT.
SUCH THINGS NEVER HAPPEN ANYWHERE ELSE.

ARRIVED AT VIENNA, THEY VISIT THE THEATRE. A GENTLEMAN THERE, UNOBTRUSIVELY PAYS THEM GREAT ATTENTION.

VIENNA.

SCENE—SHOP, VIENNA.

JONES TO BROWN—"WHAT DO YOU SAY?"

BROWN (WHO SEES THAT ROBINSON IS BENT UPON MAKING A "MAGNIFICENT ADDITION" TO HIMSELF, AND THAT IT IS USELESS TO EXPOSTULATE).—"OH, I THINK IT IS SPLENDID; AND IF YOU WILL ONLY APPEAR IN IT IN PALL MALL, WHEN WE GET HOME AGAIN, YOU WILL MAKE A SENSATION."

THEY VISIT THE PICTURE GALLERIES.

THAT MAN IN THE DOORWAY SEEMS TO TAKE A GREAT INTEREST IN THEIR MOVEMENTS.

VIENNA.

THE PROMENADE.
BROWN THINKS IT IS THE SAME MAN! WHAT CAN HE WANT?

THE PUBLIC GARDEN.
THERE HE WAS AGAIN! JONES SUGGESTED THAT PERHAPS IT WAS A GOVERNMENT OFFICIAL, WHO TOOK THEM
FOR LIBERTY, EQUALITY, AND FRATERNITY.

VIENNA

NO SOONER DID THEY TAKE THEIR PLACES AT THE TABLE D'HOTE TO DINE, THAN BROWN FELL BACK IN HIS CHAIR. THERE COULD BE NO DOUBT ABOUT IT—HE WAS BETTER DRESSED THAN BEFORE—BUT IT WAS THE SAME MAN!—HE MUST BE A SPY!

JONES AT THE OPERA ABROAD.

HOW UNLIKE JONES AT THE OPERA AT HOME.

VIENNA TO PRAGUE.

"JUST TEN MINUTES TO DRESS, BREAKFAST, AND GET TO THE TRAIN."

WALLENSTEIN'S HORSE.

"THE HEAD, NECK, LEGS, AND PART OF THE BODY HAVE BEEN REPAIRED—ALL THE REST IS THE REAL HORSE."—*From speech of the young woman who showed the animal.*

PRAGUE.

A "KNEIPE" AT PRAGUE

ROBINSON IS SO CONFUSED WITH RAPID TRAVELLING, THAT HE ADDRESSES A WAITER IN THREE LANGUAGES AT ONCE.
"KELLNER!—MITTAGS-ESSEN POUR TROIS—PRESTO PRESTO—AND—WAITER!—SODA WATER—COL COGNAC—GESCHWIND!"

PRAGUE TO COLOGNE.

TABLE D'HOTE, PRAGUE.

"PASSPORTS!"—"THAT'S THE SIXTH TIME WE HAVE BEEN WOKE UP," GROANED ROBINSON.

RHINELAND AGAIN.

DUSSELDORF.
BROWN *loq.*—I HAVE LEFT MY BAG BEHIND!

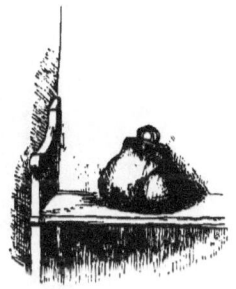

MINDEN.
HERE IS THE BAG.

HOW BROWN WAS SEATED BETWEEN TWO SOLDIERS, AND HOW THEY WOULD EXAMINE EACH OTHER'S SWORDS, AND HOW THOSE FEARFUL WEAPONS WERE FLASHING ABOUT, OFTEN WITHIN AN INCH OF B.'S NOSE; AND HOW (BEING OF A MILD AND PEACEFUL DISPOSITION), B. WAS KEPT THEREBY IN A CONSTANT STATE OF UNEASINESS.

BELGIUM.

EYE OF THE GOVERNMENT; AS KEPT UPON THE TRAVELLERS, DURING THEIR STAY IN THE AUSTRIAN DOMINIONS.—*Drawn from the haunted imagination of Brown.*

THEIR LAST REPAST IN FOREIGN PARTS.

TIME AND TRAIN WAIT FOR NO MAN.

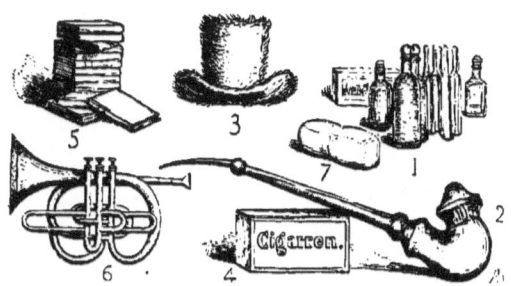

ARTICLES PURCHASED BY ROBINSON.

1. Eau de Cologne. 2. Pipe; (never smoked.) 3. Hat; (never worn, and found decidedly in the way.) 4. Cigars; (stopped at Custom House.) 5. Tauchnitz Editions; (also seized.) 6. Carpet & pistols; (bought in Germany with the intention of learning to play upon it some day.) 7. Gloves; (purchased at Venice, a great bargain, and found utterly worthless.)

OLD ENGLAND.

Sic (k) Transit

Gloria Mundi!

www.ingramcontent.com/pod-product-compliance
Lightning Source LLC
Chambersburg PA
CBHW030312170426
43202CB00009B/981